drive

These quotations were gathered lovingly but unscientifically over several years and/or contributed by many friends or acquaintances. Some arrived, and survived in our files, on scraps of paper and may therefore be imperfectly worded or attributed. To the authors, contributors and original sources, our thanks, and where appropriate, our apologies.—The editors

CREDITS

Compiled by Dan Zadra
Designed by Steve Potter

ISBN: 1-932319-41-7

Printed in China

Following the light of the sun,
we left the Old World.

CHRISTOPHER COLUMBUS

BELIEVE
IN SOMETHING BIG.
YOUR LIFE IS WORTH A
NOBLE MOTIVE.

WALTER ANDERSON

I want to
put a ding
in the
universe.

STEVE JOBS

There are two ways to face the future. One is with apprehension; the other is with anticipation.

JIM ROHN

WE ARE CALLED TO BE

ARCHITECTS OF THE FUTURE,

NOT ITS VICTIMS.

BUCKMINSTER FULLER

Man is a
creature of
hope and
invention,
both of which
belie the idea
that things
cannot be
changed.

DAN ZADRA

CONCERN SHOULD DRIVE US INTO ACTION
AND NOT INTO A DEPRESSION.

KAREN HORNEY

Decide
to make a
dramatic
move
that will
change
everything
for the
better.

KOBI YAMADA

How to begin the

journey? You need

only take the first

step. When? There

is always now.

GEORGE LEONARD

Hire good people

and let them

be good.

CLAY RAMSEY

WHAT DRIVES THESE
PEOPLE
IS NOT A DESIRE
FOR POWER
BUT A DESIRE TO HAVE A POSITIVE
INFLUENCE ON
THEIR WORKPLACE AND
THE WORLD.

DARWIN SANOY

Work has to include our deepest values and passions and feelings and commitments, or it's not work, it's just a job.

MATTHEW FOX

Don't believe that winning

is really everything. It's more

important to stand for something.

If we don't stand for something,

what do we win?

JOSEPH LANE KIRKLAND

Be fanatics.

When it comes

to being, doing and

dreaming the best,

be maniacs.

A.M. ROSENTHAL

There must be bands of enthusiasts for everything on earth—fanatics who share a vocabulary, a batch of technical skills and equipment, and perhaps a vision of some single slice of the beauty and mystery of things.

ANNIE DILLARD

My passions were
all gathered together
like fingers that
made a fist.
Drive is considered
aggression today;
I knew it then
as purpose.

People say
don't take business
personally—but
that's my work,
my sweat, my time
away from my
family—how can that
not be personal?

ELAINE BRANSON

NOT KNOWING IT ALL
IS NO EXCUSE NOT TO START.

JUDY COLUMBUS

As long as you can start,

you are all right.

The juice will come.

ERNEST HEMINGWAY

MAKE SURE EVERYBODY'S

ON BOARD THE TRAIN.

MIKE KRZYZEWSKI

Get everyone in the

flow. Your flow is

as tangible and real

as any locomotive,

and just as powerful.

ROBERT GENN

Even when we are not in charge, we can act. Even when we are not formally designated leaders, we can lead.

GEOFFREY BELLMAN

Imagine if everyone in the company had the courage and the confidence and the risk-seeking profile that we associate with leaders. That's the direction every company must head.

CHANCE DUNCAN

YOU OWE IT TO US
TO GET ON
WITH WHAT YOU'RE
GOOD AT.

W.H. AUDEN

If you practice an art,

be proud of it and

make it proud of you.

It may break your heart,

but it will fill your heart

before it breaks it:

It will make you a person

in your own right.

MAXWELL ANDERSON

LEADERSHIP IS LIKE A RACE CAR.
IF YOU WANT TO WIN,
YOU HAVE TO DRIVE IT,
NOT JUST GO FOR THE RIDE.

BUTCH HOLMBERG

If we aren't customer driven, our cars won't be either.

AUTO INDUSTRY EXECUTIVE

COMPETITION IS A WAY
OF LIFE. IF YOU DON'T
HAVE A REALLY TOUGH
COMPETITOR, YOU
OUGHT TO INVENT ONE.

WILLIAM SMITHBURG

I HAVE BEEN UP AGAINST

TOUGH COMPETITION

ALL MY LIFE. I WOULDN'T

KNOW HOW TO GET

ALONG WITHOUT IT.

WALT DISNEY

When your organization operates like a strong family, you can't be knocked out by one punch.

MIKE KRZYZEWSKI

If you stick together

and keep working at it,

in the last analysis you win.

They've got to kill us

a hundred times.

All we have to do

is kill them once.

FRED SMITH

COMMITTED PEOPLE
  RULE OUT EXCUSES.

J O H N   E .   N E W M A N

Some people have thousands of reasons why they cannot do what they want to, when all they need is one reason why they can.

MARY FRANCES BERRY

Don't "take care," take a risk!

DENIS WAITLEY

Fall down. Make a mess. Break something occasionally. Know that your mistakes are your own unique way of getting to where you need to be. And remember that the story is never over.

CONAN O'BRIEN

I AM OLD ENOUGH

TO KNOW THAT VICTORY

IS OFTEN A THING DEFERRED.

WHAT IS AT THE SUMMIT

OF COURAGE, I THINK,

IS FREEDOM.

THE FREEDOM THAT COMES

WITH THE KNOWLEDGE

THAT NO EARTHLY THING

CAN BREAK YOU.

PAULA GIDDINGS

If you break your neck,
if you have nothing to eat,
if your house is on fire,
then you've got a problem.
Everything else
is just inconvenience.

ROBERT FULGHUM

A crisis is
a terrible
thing to
waste.

PAUL ROMER

ASSUME THAT WHATEVER SITUATION YOU ARE FACING AT THE MOMENT, HOWEVER DIFFICULT IT MAY BE, IS EXACTLY THE RIGHT SITUATION YOU NEED TO ULTIMATELY BE SUCCESSFUL. THIS SITUATION HAS BEEN SENT.

BRIAN TRACY

FAILURE IS A NORMAL,
NATURAL WAY OF
MAPPING THE UNKNOWN.

JACK MATSON

Don't think of it

as failure;

think of it as

time-released success.

ROBERT ORBEN

TO FINISH FIRST,
YOU MUST FIRST FINISH.

RICK MEARS

Stopping a piece of work just because it's hard, either emotionally or imaginatively, is a bad idea. Sometimes you have to go on when you don't feel like it.

STEPHEN KING

Most people give up just when they're about to achieve success. They quit on the one yard line. They give up the last minute of the game, one foot from a winning touchdown.

ROSS PEROT

THE TRAGEDY OF LIFE

IS NOT THAT WE LOSE,

BUT THAT WE ALMOST WIN.

HEYWOOD BROWN

YOU MAY FORGET
HOW YOU
BEHAVED
WHEN THE GOING
GOT TOUGH,
BUT OTHERS WON'T.

MARK BURNETT

I believe that the details of our lives will be forgotten by most, but the emotion, the spirit, will linger with those who shared it and be part of them forever.

LIV ULLMAN

LIFE IS TOO LONG NOT TO DO IT RIGHT.

DIANE DEACON

Ask yourselves,

"How long are we

going to work to make

our dreams come true?"

I suggest you answer,

"As long as it takes."

JIM ROHN

WE WILL BE
VICTORIOUS
IF WE HAVE NOT
FORGOTTEN
HOW TO LEARN.

ROSA LUXEMBURG

It is not the strongest of the species that survive, nor even the most intelligent, but the one most responsive to change.

CHARLES DARWIN

THE HARDEST THING TO BELIEVE
WHEN YOU'RE YOUNG
IS THAT PEOPLE WILL FIGHT
TO STAY IN A RUT,
BUT NOT TO GET OUT OF IT.

ELLEN GLASGOW

If you keep following

your own footprints,

you will end up

where you began,

but if you stretch yourself

you will flourish.

MICHAEL ALTSHULER

THE BAD NEWS IS TIME FLIES.

THE GOOD NEWS IS YOU'RE THE PILOT.

MICHAEL ALTSHULER

I'M STILL READY TO GO TO THE MOON, IF THEY'LL TAKE ME.

WALTER CRONKITE

I would rather be ashes than dust; I would rather that my spark should burn out in a brilliant blaze than it should be stifled by dry-rot...the proper function of man is to live, not to exist; I shall not waste my days in trying to prolong them; I shall USE my time.

JACK LONDON

The greatest
thing is to
push on
through, and
say at the end,
"The dream
is true."

EDWIN MARKHAM